FERRUCCIO LAVIANI

daab

Introduction

Architecture

Interior & Retails

Product Design

Exhibitions

Stand Design

The choice to become an architect was accidental, just like many of the other choices in my life.

After going to the Technical Institute for Craftsmen Lute makers and Wood in Cremona, I enrolled in the Faculty of Architecture of the Milan Polytechnic where I followed courses with Achille Castiglioni and Marco Zanuso. After university, I enrolled in the Polytechnic School of Design, more because I didn't want to work than for a real love for the subject. This led me to work in the Studio De Lucchi, which I left in 1991 to open my own company.

Throughout these years, I've gone from Memphis to Minimalism, trying each time to take the best without being dominated and, within the possible limits, trying to be as sincere as possible in the relationship with the project. The influence of Michele de Lucchi, collaboration with Castiglioni, the close friendship with Rodolfo Dordoni and meeting designers and architects from all over the world is what continues to focus my view of things and is the starting point for my projects, just as my customers, friends and family or ordinary people are. Castiglioni said, "In particular, you must always be inquisitive," and if, at first sight, it seems simplistic, at times being inquisitive implies a certain effort but is a *leitmotiv* which I often try to repeat to myself and not forget.

I've never had a personal iconography or a brand name – and I really don't want it, i.e., I'd be the first to be bored with myself – but I always hope that people are happily struck by the fact that, for the umpteenth time, 'something' has been designed by me, whether it's a shop, an object or anything else which stimulates a feeling. By using simple resources as plain geometric shapes and strong colours I want to create powerful images.

Part of my work over almost 25 years is collected in this book. Reading the historical and 'stylistic' path is like looking at myself in the mirror once more and trying to look lucidly at the good, and less good, things that I've done.

As I'm not nostalgic though - next please!

Die Wahl Architekt zu werden, traf ich rein zufällig sowie im übrigen die meisten Entscheidungen in meinem Leben.

Nachdem ich das Technische Institut für Herstellung von Saiteninstrumenten und Holzhandwerk in Cremona besucht habe, schrieb ich mich an der Architekturfakultät des Mailänder Polytechnikums ein, wo ich unter anderem Kurse bei Achille Castiglioni und Marco Zanuso belegte. Nach Abschluss der Universität entschied ich, eher aufgrund mangelnder Lust zu arbeiten, als aufgrund einer wahren Schwärmerei für die Disziplin, auf das Design Polytechnikum zu gehen. Dies führte dazu, daß ich bis zur Eröffnung meines eigenen Büros 1991 im Studio De Lucchi arbeitete.

In all diesen Jahren geriet ich von Memphis zum Minimalismus, wobei ich ständig versuchte, jeweils das Beste herauszuholen, ohne jedoch hörig zu sein, sondern möglichst ehrlich zu entwerfen. Der Einfluss von Michele de Lucchi, die Zusammenarbeit mit Castiglioni, die Freundschaft mit Rodolfo Dordoni und die Bekanntschaft mit Designern und Architekten aus der ganzen Welt schärft dauernd meinen Blick und gibt den Anstoß zu meinen Projekten, so wie auch Kunden, Freunde, Verwandte oder ganz gewöhnliche Leute. „Du musst vor allem immer neugierig sein" sagte mir Castiglioni und wenn dieser Satz auch auf den ersten Blick recht simpel klingt, ist Neugier manchmal sehr anstrengend. Trotzdem stellt sie ein Leitmotiv dar, das ich versuche, oft zu wiederholen und nie zu vergessen.

Ich hatte nie ein eigenes Label, eine Marke. Und ehrlich gesagt, möchte ich es auch gar nicht beziehungsweise wäre ich der erste, der von sich selbst gelangweilt wäre. Ich hoffe aber immer, daß sich jemand darüber freut, zum x-ten Male zu entdecken, daß „etwas" von mir entworfen wurde, sei es ein Geschäft, ein Objekt oder irgend etwas anderes, das ein Gefühl hervorruft. Mit dem Gebrauch einfacher Mittel, wie reine Geometrien oder starke Farben, möchte ich kraftvolle Bilder erzeugen.

Das Buch umfasst einen Teil meiner, in fast 25 Jahren, realisierten Arbeiten. In ihnen den historischen und „stilistischen" Verlauf zu lesen, ist, wie mich im Spiegel zu betrachten und zu versuchen, die guten oder weniger guten Dinge, die ich realisiert habe, klar zu betrachten.

Ich bin nicht nostalgisch und deshalb: Next!

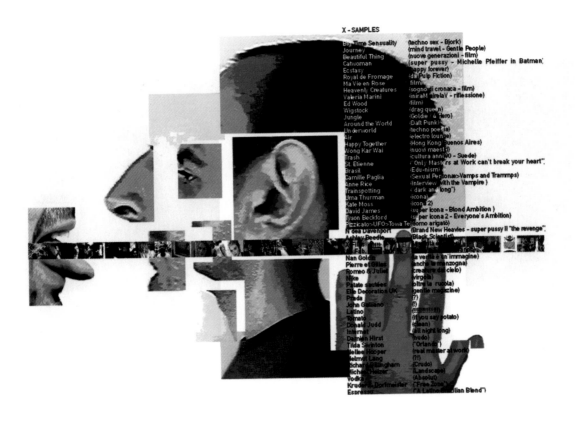

X - SAMPLES

Big Time Sensuality (techno sex - Bjork)
Journey (mind travel - Gentle People)
Beautiful Thing (nuove generazioni - film)
Catwoman (super pussy - Michelle Pfeiffer in Batman)
Ecstasy (happy forever)
Royal de Fromage (da Pulp Fiction)
Ma Vie en Rose (film)
Heavenly Creatures (sogno di cronaca - film)
Valeria Marini (iniraM airelaV - riflessione)
Ed Wood (film)
Wigstock (drag queen)
Jungle (Goldie / 4 Hero)
Around the World (Daft Punk)
Underworld (techno poesia)
Air (electro lounge)
Happy Together (Hong Kong Buenos Aires)
Wong Kar Wai (nuovi maestri)
Trash (cultura anni 90 - Suede)
St. Etienne ("Only Masters at Work can't break your heart")
Brasil (Edu-nismi)
Camille Paglia (Sexual Personae>Vamps and Tramps)
Anne Rice (Interview with the Vampire)
Trainspotting (dark and long)
Uma Thurman (icona)
Kate Moss (icona 2)
Tyson Beckford (super icona - Blond Ambition)
David James (super icona 2 - Everyone's Ambition)
Pizzicato>UFO>Towa Tei (domo arigató)
N'dea Davenport (Brand New Heavies – super pussy II "the revenge")
Ashley Beedle (Black Scientist)

Nan Goldin (la verità è un'immagine)
Pierre et Gilles (anche la menzogna)
Romeo & Juliet (creature dal cielo)
Nike (virgola)
Patate sautées (oltre la rucola)
Elle Decoration UK (gentle magazine)
Prada (?)
John Galliano (!)
Latino (!!!!!!!!!!!!)
Tomato (if you say potato)
Donald Judd (clean)
Internet (all night long)
Damien Hirst (nudo)
Tilda Swinton ("Orlando")
Nellee Hooper (real master at work)
Helmut Lang (?!)
Richard Billingham (Crudo)
Michael Heizer (Landscape)
Vodka (Absolut)
Kruder & Dorfmeister ("Free Zone")
Espresso ("A Latino Italian Blend")

La decisión de ser arquitecto la tomé por casualidad, como ha ocurrido con la gran mayoría de las decisiones de mi vida.

Después de frecuentar el Instituto Técnico para la Artesanía de Instrumentos de Cuerda y de Madera en Cremona, me inscribí en la Facultad de Arquitectura del Politécnico de Milán donde cursé estudios con Achille Castiglioni y Marco Zanuso, entre otros. Una vez terminada la universidad, más por las pocas ganas de trabajar que por una verdadera pasión por la disciplina, me inscribí en la Escuela Politécnica de Diseño lo que me llevó a trabajar en el estudio De Lucchi, del cual salí en 1991 para abrir mi propio estudio.

En todos estos años he pasado desde Memphis hasta el minimalismo, buscando cada vez escoger lo mejor pero sin someterme, y buscando, dentro de lo posible, ser lo más honesto posible en mi relación con cada proyecto. La influencia de Michele de Lucchi, las colaboraciones con Castiglioni, la amistad de Rodolfo Dordoni y el conocer diseñadores de casi todo el mundo es lo que sigue orientando mi visión de las cosas e inspirando mis proyectos, como también los clientes, amigos y familiares, las personas comunes. "Sobretodo, debes siempre ser curioso" decía Castiglioni y si, a primera vista, parece una frase simplista a veces ser curioso implica cierto esfuerzo, pero es un *leitmotiv* que trato de repetirme a menudo para no olvidarlo.

Nunca he tenido una iconografia o una marca de fábrica —y sinceramente tampoco lo quisiera pues de esta manera sería el primero en aburrirme de mí mismo— sin embargo, siempre espero que la gente quede felizmente impresionada por el hecho de descubrir que por enésima vez una "cierta cosa" ha sido diseñada por mí, ya sea una tienda, un objeto o cualquier otra cosa que estimule cualquier sentimiento. Con el uso de recursos simples así como también de geometrías y colores fuertes trato de crear imágenes de gran impacto.

En este libro se reúne una recopilación de mis trabajos realizados durante casi 25 años. Leer aquí mi trayectoria histórica y estilística es como volver a verme en el espejo y tratar de ver con lucidez las cosas buenas, o menos buenas, que he realizado.

No soy nostálgico, por lo tanto: al próximo!

Le choix de devenir architecte s'est produit un peu par hasard, comme du reste une grande partie des choix de mon existence.

Après avoir fréquenté l'Institut Technique de l'Artisanat Luthier et du Bois de Crémone, je me suis inscrit à la faculté d'architecture de l'Institut Polytechnique de Milan, où j'ai suivi, entre autres, des cours avec Achille Castiglioni et Marco Zanuso. Après avoir terminé l'université, plus par non-envie de travailler que par véritable engouement pour la discipline, je me suis inscrit à l'Ecole Polytechnique de Design qui m'a amené à travailler dans le cabinet De Lucchi, que j'ai quitté en 1991 pour ouvrir mon propre cabinet.

Durant toutes ces années je suis passé de Memphis au Minimalisme, cherchant à chaque fois à en prendre le meilleur sans toutefois en être succube et cherchant, dans la limite du possible, à être le plus sincère possible dans le rapport avec le projet. L'influence de Michele de Lucchi, les collaborations avec Castiglioni, l'amitié fraternelle avec Rodolfo Dordoni et la connaissance de designers et d'architectes d'un peu partout dans le monde est ce qui continue à focaliser ma vision des choses et représente le départ de mes projets, comme le sont également les clients, les amis et parents ou les gens ordinaires. "Par-dessus tout, tu dois toujours être curieux" disait Castiglioni et si, à première vue, cela semble une phrase toute faite, parfois être curieux implique un certain effort, mais c'est un *leitmotiv* que j'essaie de me répéter souvent et de ne pas oublier.

Je n'ai jamais eu une iconographie personnelle ni une marque de fabrique - et sincèrement je ne le voudrais même pas, ou alors je serais le premier à être ennuyé de moi-même - mais j'espère toujours que les gens seront positivement frappés en découvrant que pour la enième fois un "quelque chose " a été projeté par moi, que ce soit un magasin, un objet ou n'importe quoi d'autre qui stimule quelque sentiment. En utilisant des moyens simples comme des géométries pures ou des couleurs fortes, je veux créer des images vigoureuses.

Dans ce livre est rassemblée une partie des travaux que j'ai réalisés en près de 25 ans. En lire le parcours historique et «stylistique» est comme me regarder dans un miroir et essayer de voir lucidement ce que j'ai réalisé de bon, ou de moins bon.

Je ne suis pas nostalgique, alors : Next!

La scelta di essere architetto è avvenuta un po' per caso come del resto gran parte delle scelte della mia vita.

Dopo aver frequentato l'Istituto Tecnico per l'Artigianato Liutario e del Legno di Cremona mi sono iscritto alla Facoltà di Architettura del Politecnico di Milano dove tra gli altri ho seguito corsi con Achille Castiglioni e Marco Zanuso. Terminata l'Università, più per la non voglia di lavorare che per una vera infatuazione della disciplina, mi sono iscritto alla Scuola Politecnica di Design che mi ha portato a lavorare nello Studio De Lucchi che ho lasciato nel 1991 per aprire il mio proprio studio.

In tutti questi anni sono passato da Memphis al Minimalismo cercando tutte le volte di prenderne il meglio senza però esserne succube e cercando, nei limiti del possibile, di essere il più sincero possibile nel rapporto con il progetto. L'influenza di Michele de Lucchi, le collaborazioni con Castiglioni, l'amicizia con Rodolfo Dordoni e la conoscenza di designer di un po' tutte le parti del mondo è ciò che continua a focalizzare la mia visione delle cose e lo spunto ai miei progetti, così pure come lo sono i clienti, amici e familiari o le persone comuni. "Sopratutto devi sempre essere curioso" diceva Castiglioni e se, a prima vista ,sembra una frase semplicistica a volte l'esserlo implica un certo sforzo ma è un *leitmotiv* che cerco di ripetermi spesso e di non dimenticare.

Non ho mai avuto un'iconografia mia o un marchio di fabbrica - e sinceramente non lo vorrei nemmeno oppure sarei il primo ad essere annoiato di me stesso - ma spero sempre che la gente rimanga felicemente colpita dal fatto di scoprire che per l'ennesima volta un "qualche cosa " sia stato progettato da me, sia un negozio, un oggetto o qualsiasi altra cosa che stimoli un qualsiasi sentimento. Con l'uso di risorse semplici come pure geometrie e colori forti cerco di creare immagini di notevole impatto.

In questo libro sono raccolti parte dei miei lavori realizzati in quasi 25 anni. Leggerne il percorso storico e "stilistico" è come riguardarmi allo specchio e cercare di vedere lucidamente le cose buone, o meno, che ho realizzato.

Non sono nostalgico perciò: Next !

ARCHITECTURE

INTERIOR & RETAILS

PRODUCT DESIGN

EXHIBITIONS

STAND DESIGN

KARTELL
SHOWROOM
Milan, Italy | 1997

PRIVATE RESIDENCE
INTERIOR DESIGN
Milan, Italy | 1998

KARTELL
MUSEUM
Milan, Italy | 1999

FLOS
SHOWROOM
Copenhagen, Denmark | 2002

PIPER HEIDSIECK
"PAVILLON 1921" HEADQUARTERS
WORK IN PROGRESS
Reims, France | 2007

GRAND HOTEL BORDEAUX
FASHION AVENUE
WORK IN PROGRESS
Bordeaux, France | 2007

PIOMBO
CONCEPT | CORPORATE IDENTITY
Milan, Italy | 2000

PIOMBO

SOCIETY LIMONTA
FLAGSHIP RENOVATION
Milan, Italy | 2005

DOLCE & GABBANA
BOUTIQUES
world-wide | since 2000

DOLCE & GABBANA
HEADQUARTERS
Milan, Italy | 2002

BAR MARTINI
Dolce & Gabbana
Milan, Italy | 2003

METROPOL
SPACE FOR FASHION SHOWS
Dolce & Gabbana
Milan, Italy | 2005

DOLCE & GABBANA
BOUTIQUE UOMO & BARBER SHOP
Milan, Italy | 2003

ANTONINI
CONCEPT | CORPORATE IDENTITY
Tokyo, Japan | 2006

LA RINASCENTE
PERFUMERY | ACCESSORIES AREA
Padua, Italy | 2006

GOLD
RESTAURANT | BISTRO | BAR | PASTRY SHOP
Dolce & Gabbana
Milan, Italy | 2006

ROMEO
LIBRARY
Memphis | 1987

SEBASTIANO | PAOLA

Imel | 1991 - 1992

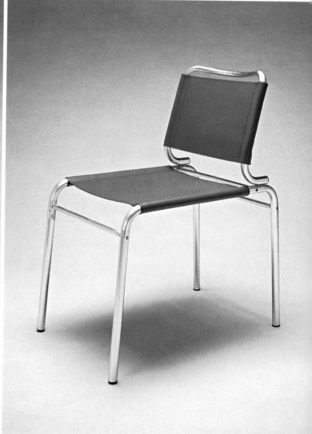

SOLANGE SERIES
Schopenhauer
Fontana Arte Group | 1997 - 2007

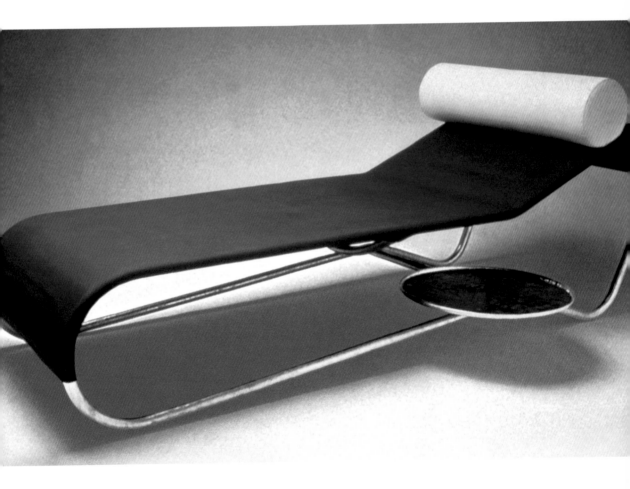

40/80
with Achille Castiglioni
Moroso | 1999

NASSA | PALERMO
SHIVA | CRASH
Emmemobili | 1994 - 2007

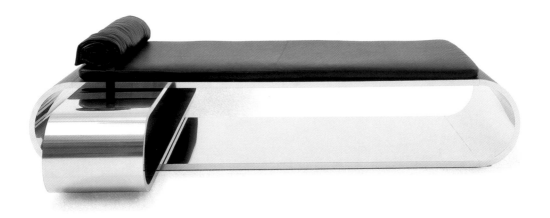

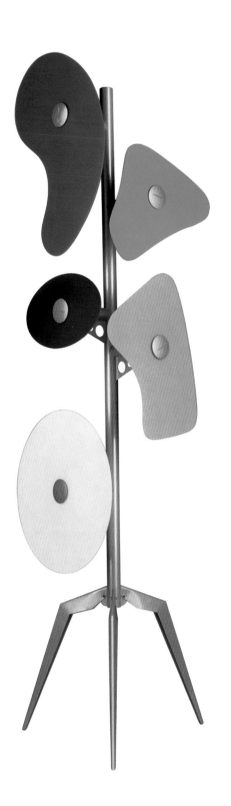

BIT | ORBITAL | DOLMEN
Foscarini | 1993 | 1992 | 1996

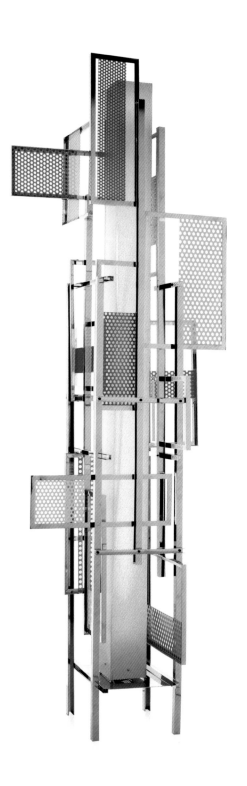

TEOREMA | ARETHA
Foscarini | 2005 | 2006

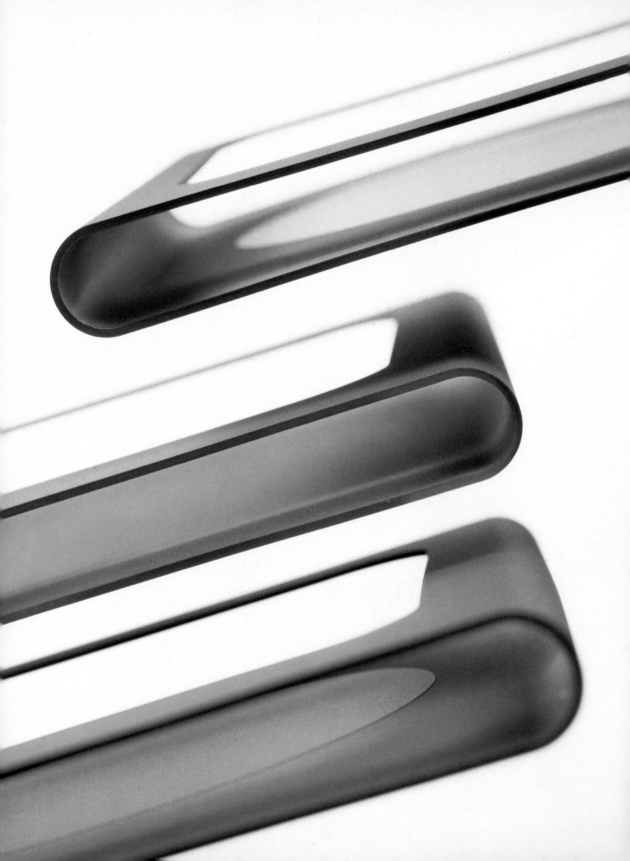

HABIBY
TRAY
Zani & Zani | 2001

FL/Y | EASY
Kartell | 2002

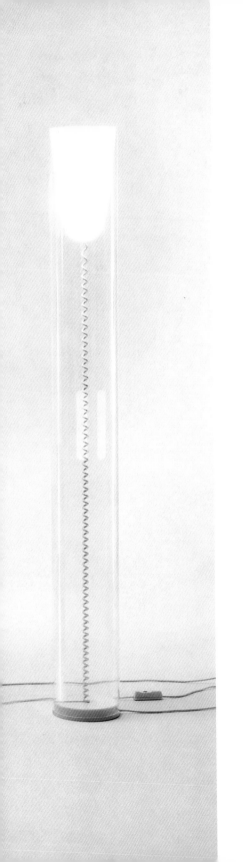

TOOBE
Kartell | 2007

E'
Kartell | 2006

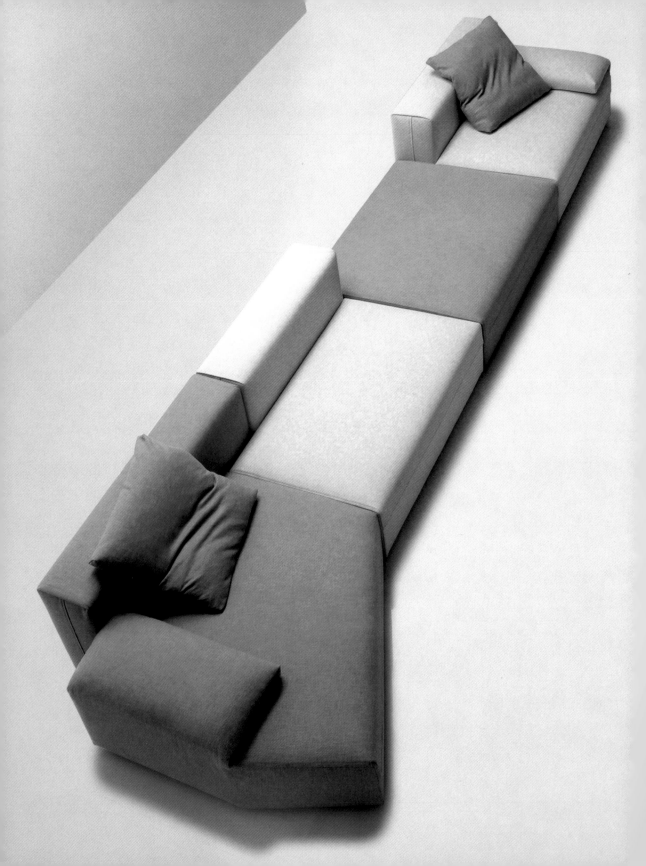

FREESTYLE
Molteni & C. | 2005

QUADRANTE
Dada Alta Cucina | 1999

VELA QUADRA | HI LINE
Dada Alta Cucina | 2003 | 2005

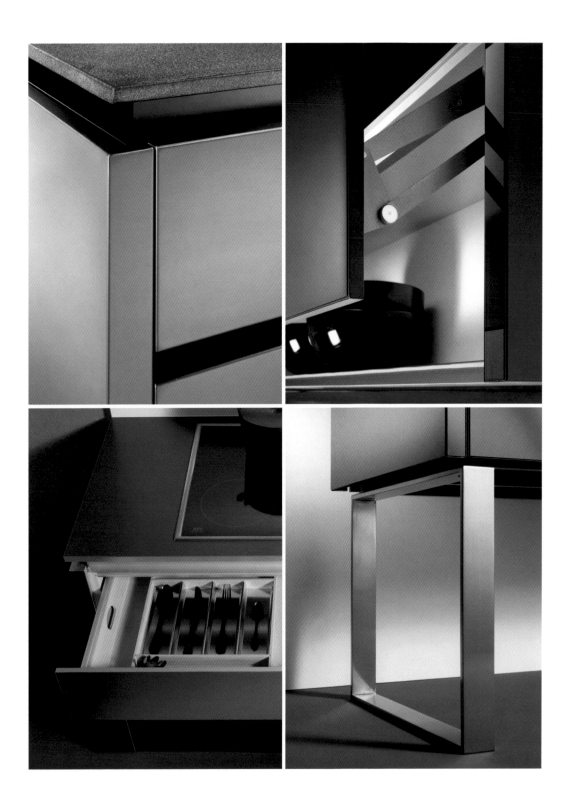

VICO MAGISTRETTI
with Achille Castiglioni
Client: Cosmit
Salone del Mobile | 1997
Milan, Italy

ABITARE ITALIA
Client: Italian Ambassy
Brasilia, Brazil | 1996

MOROSO
SHOWROOM SET UP
Milan, Italy | 1997

BRUNO MUNARI
Client: Cosmit
Milan, Italy | 1998

ONE NIGHT IN *heaven*

ONE NIGHT IN HEAVEN
SHOWROOM SET UP | GRAPHICS
Client: Moroso
Milan, Italy | 1998

40/80
SHOWROOM SET UP
Client: Moroso
Milan, Italy | 1999

COOK SPACE
Client: Dada Alta Cucina
Abitare il tempo
Verona, Italy | 1999

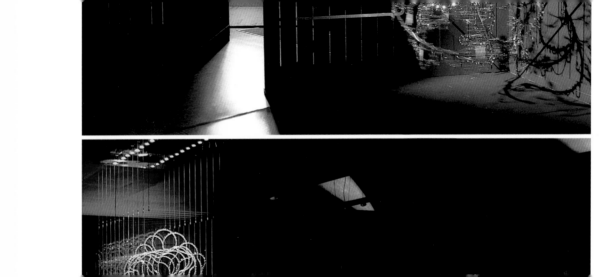

DE PADOVA
SHOWROOM SET UP
Milan, Italy | 1997 - 2005

DESIGN ANTONIO CITTERIO CON TOAN NGUYEN

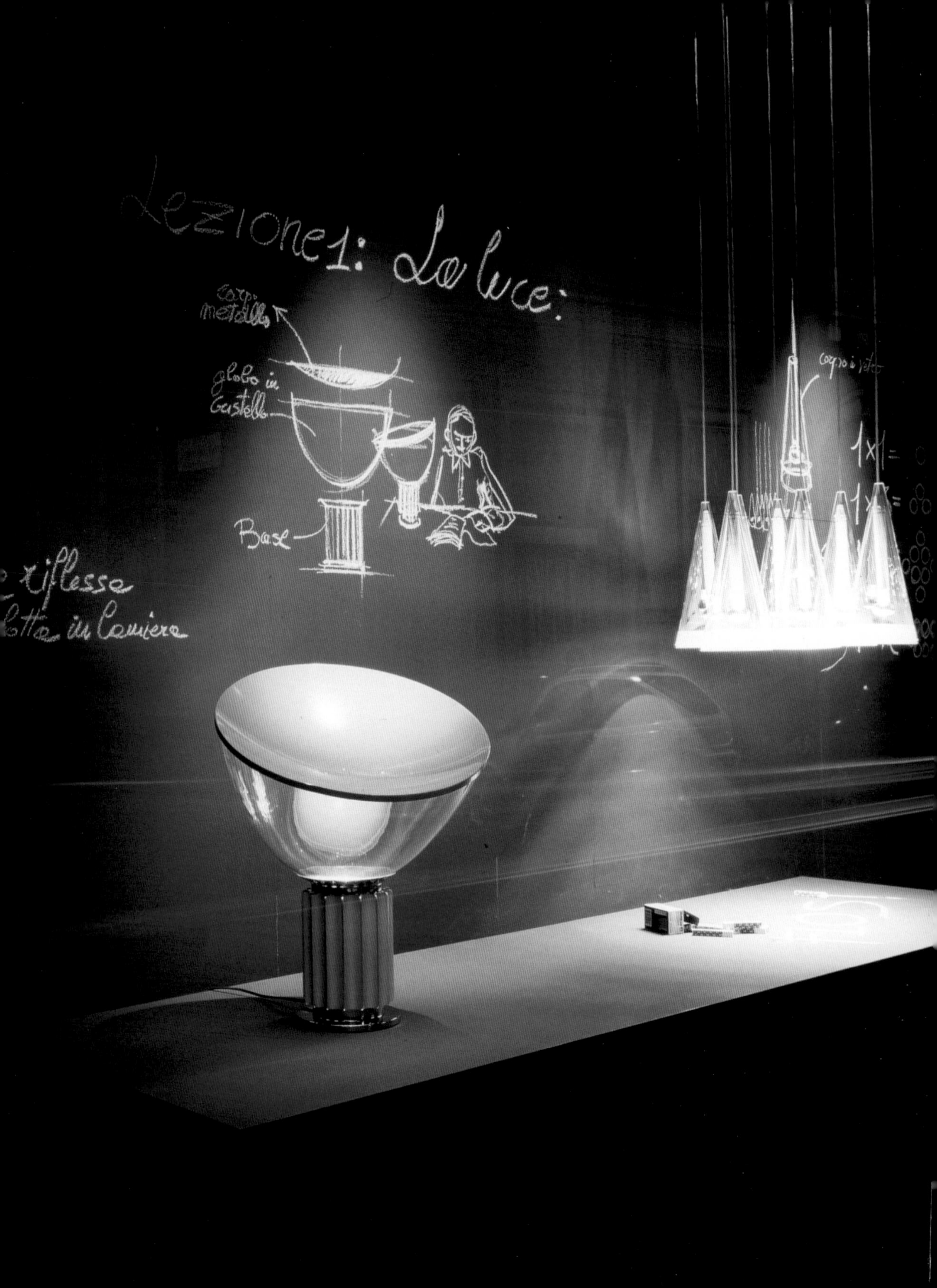
Lezione1: La luce:
globo in
Base
riflesse

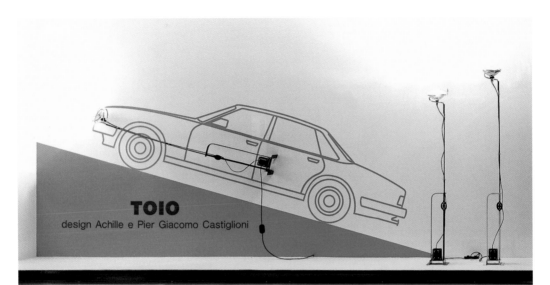

TOIO
design Achille e Pier Giacomo Castiglioni

KARTELL
SHOP WINDOWS | SHOWROOM SET UP | GRAPHICS
world-wide | 1997 - 2007

Kartell

I 💡 Kartell

Au 242 Boulevard St. Germain, dans le showroom Kartell complètement rénové, la présentation des nouvelles collections signées Ferruc
Cocktail jeudi, 26 janvier 2006 - A partir de 18h00 jusqu'à 21h00 - Kartell, 242 boulevard Saint Germain 75007 Paris

Kartel

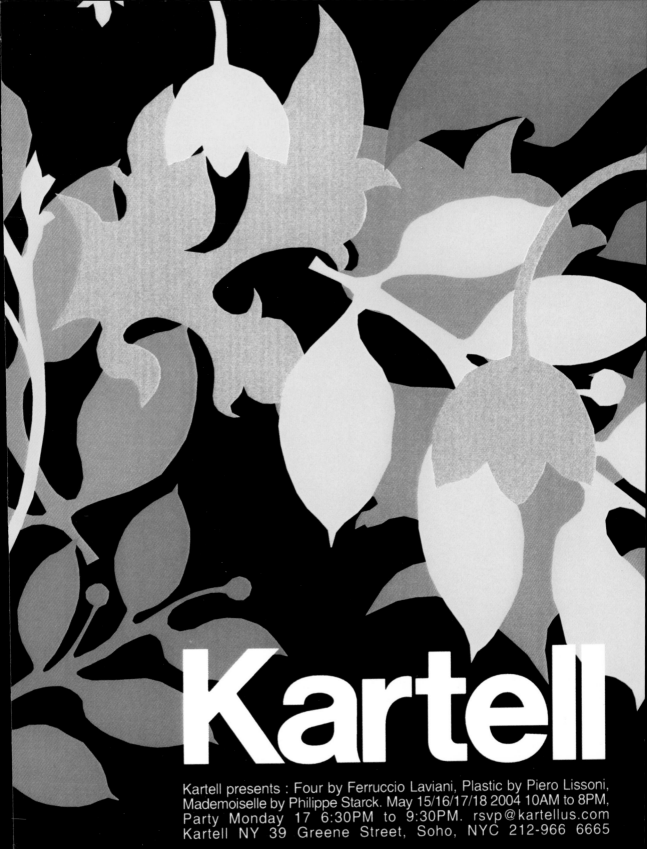

Kartell

Kartell presents : Four by Ferruccio Laviani, Plastic by Piero Lissoni,
Mademoiselle by Philippe Starck. May 15/16/17/18 2004 10AM to 8PM,
Party Monday 17 6:30PM to 9:30PM. rsvp@kartellus.com
Kartell NY 39 Greene Street, Soho, NYC 212-966 6665

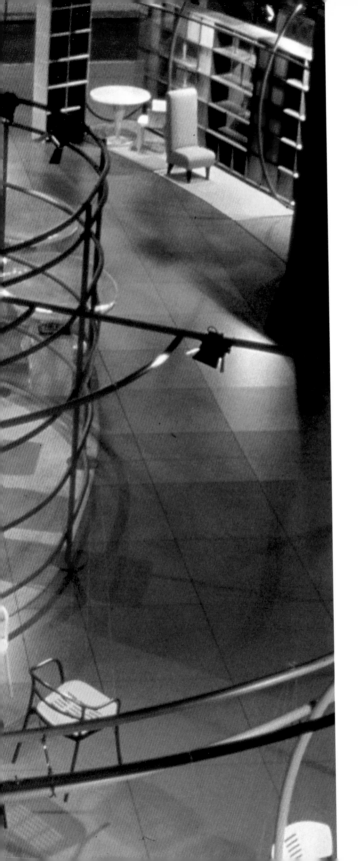

KARTELL
STAND | Salone del Mobile
Milan, Italy | 1993

KARTELL
STAND | Salone del Mobile
Milan, Italy | 1994

KARTELL
STAND | Salone del Mobile
Milan, Italy | 1995

KARTELL
STAND | Salone del Mobile
Milan, Italy | 1996

KARTELL
STAND | Salone del Mobile
Milan, Italy | 1998

EMMEMOBILI
STAND | GRAPHICS
Salone del Mobile
Milan, Italy | 1997 - 2004

MOROSO
STAND | Salone del Mobile
Milan, Italy | 2000

FLOS
STAND | Euroluce
Milan, Italy | 2000

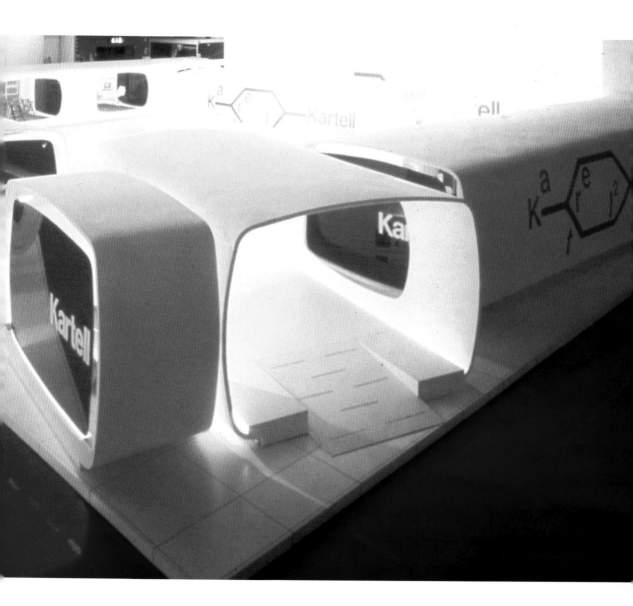

KARTELL
STAND | Salone del Mobile
Milan, Italy | 2001

FLOS
STAND | Euroluce
Milan, Italy | 2001

FLOS
STAND | Light and Building
Frankfurt, Germany | 2002

KARTELL
STAND | Salone del Mobile
Milan, Italy | 2002

FLOS**CONTR**

FL[

anta[

IRRESISTIBLY CREATED IN EVERY OBSERVER. LIGHT ADDS TO THE ATTRACTIVE ATMOSPHERES THAT
THE SHADOWS CREATED BY EVERY OBJECT BECAUSE LIGHT ADDS TO THE ATTRACTIVE ATMOSPHERES THAT
MEN MAKE SO MUCH USE OF LIGHT AND SHADOWS." REFERS TO THE ATTRACTIVE ATMOSPHERES THAT
TANIZAKI IN HIS "IN PRAISE OF SHADOWS." REFERS TO THE ATTRACTIVE ATMOSPHERES THAT
INTRODUCING SHADOWS, THE JAPANESE WRITER OUTLINES INTIMATE IN HOME INTERIORS
A SOURCE OF WELL-BEING FOR THE DAY AND SPIRIT, THAT ARE DESIRABLE IN HOME INTERIORS
AND IN PUBLIC AND WORK PLACES, THAT SHOULD ALWAYS OFFER A SENSE OF "HOMELINESS.
SPECIALIZING IN LIGHTING DOES NOT MEAN MAKING MORE LIGHT, BUT PERHAPS IT MEANS SHADING,
REESTABLISHING THE CHANGING COLOR OF NATURAL LIGHT WITH FIXTURES THAT CAN ADJUST
THE QUANTITY AND QUALITY OF NATURAL LIGHT. IT'S WORTH HAVING SHADE, NOT TO RETURN TO
OBSCURANTISM, BUT TO RESTORE OUR ABILITY TO LOOK AT THE STARS. THAT IS, OUR INNATE
ABILITY TO LET OURSELVES BE MOVED BY EVERY FORM OF LIGHT, WHETHER NATURAL OR ARTIFICIAL.
PRODUCING TECHNICAL OR DECORATIVE FIXTURES THAT ARE EFFICIENT AND THAT HAVE A GOOD
AESTHETIC DESIGN IS NOT ENOUGH. COMPANIES MUST BE ABLE TO CREATE SOFT SHADING TO
SET THE TONE FOR ATMOSPHERES THAT REFLECT VARIOUS EMOTIONAL TONALITIES. LIGHT CAN
DESIGN ARCHITECTURE, AND THEREFORE FIXTURES MUST BE DESIGNED AND ORGANIZED ON THE
BASIS OF DIRECT LIGHTING, REFLECTING, REFRACTING, AND MODULATING IN ENDLESS WAYS. SO
THAT SPACE CAN SOAK UP, AND BE SHAPED BY, A VARIETY OF CHROMATIC DENSITIES.

FLOS
STAND | Euroluce
Milan, Italy | 2003

KARTELL
STAND | Salone del Mobile
Milan, Italy | 2003

Charles Ghost
design Philippe Starck

KARTELL
STAND | Salone del Mobile
Milan, Italy | 2004

KARTELL
STAND | Salone del Mobile
Milan, Italy | 2005

KARTELL
STAND | Salone del Mobile
Milan, Italy | 2006

FLOS
STAND | Euroluce
Milan, Italy | 2005

FLOS
STAND | Salone del Mobile
Milan, Italy | 2007

KARTELL
STAND | Salone del Mobile
Milan, Italy | 2007

FOSCARINI
STAND | Euroluce
Milan, Italy | 2007

INDEX

FERRUCCIO LAVIANI
Via De Amicis 53, Milano
Tel. +39 02 89421426
Fax +39 02 89420348
info@laviani.com
www.laviani.com

Pietro Ferruccio Laviani

Born in Cremona, Italy in 1960.
Graduated in Architecture at the Milan Polytechnic in 1986.

Projects

1986   Participation in the "12 nuovi Memphis"
As one of the founders of the Solid group,
designed part of its collection.

Malobbia International: furniture collection
"Residenza sulla terra"

1986-91 Partner of Studio de Lucchi

"Techiniques discretes : le design du mobilier
italien 1980-1990", Louvre, Paris

Memphis: showroom in New York

1988-91 Partner at Oil Milan

1990   Design of Historical Section of the City
Museum of Groningen, The Netherlands with
Michele De Lucchi and Geert Koster
Realization by Alessandro Mendini

Participation in exhibition "Creativitalia" in
Tokyo

Seminars on Industrial Design at the Faculty of
Architecture at the Milan Polytechnic

Imel: stand at Salone del Mobile Milan

Presentation of silverware objects of the
"Morandotti collection" at the exhibition
"Capitali europei del Nuovo Design", Centre
Pompidou, Paris

First Folio: Logo, Sugarbowl and Fruit Dish

1991   Kartell: assignment of art direction.
Responsible for all kinds of presentations,
exhibitions, stands, sales booths and world-
wide corner and shops

Imel: Sebastiano

Bross's: art direction of photographic shooting
of general catalogue

1992   Imel: Paola

Imel: Samir

Foscarini: Orbital

Bross's: Olga

1993   Foscarini: Bit

Ravarini e Castoldi: Gardone, Corvetto

Alarossa: Rumba, Samba

Busnelli: Time

1994   Emmemobili: assignment of art direction,
Edu, Rio, Ufo, Ferro

Casakit: Aria, Frame, Spring, Bahia, Carioca

"Milan in Bar", Via della Moscova, Milan

Mito: stand at Euroluce Milan

Moroso: Malta

1995   Moroso: Simple

Emmebi: stand at Salone del Mobile Milan

Technogym: style editing of "home" catalogue

Forum Confeccoes: realization of photographic
exhibition "Welcome to Brazil", Rio de Janeiro

Mito: assignment of art direction

Itaparica, Bomfim, Olinda, Slim, Marina , stand
at Euroluce Milan

Moroso: stand at IMM Cologne, showroom in
Udine and Milan

T70: catalogue photo shooting

1996   Realization of photographic exhibition of catalogue "24 hours", Galleria S. Paulo, Sao Paulo

Presentation of the 1996/97 collection, Sao
Paulo

Presentation of the collections in Sao Paulo
and Buenos Aires for "Patrock Cox– Wannabe"

Organization of the "Melissa" collection, Mube
Sculpture Museum, Sao Paulo

Exhibition "Brazil Faz Design" during the
Salone del Mobile Milan for "Bianco & Cucco"

Memphis exhibition during the Salone del
Mobile Milan

Halifax T70: stand at Salone del Mobile Milan

Schopenhauer (Fontana Arte Group): Solange
Series, Bobo

Mito: stand at Euroluce Milan

Foscarini: Dolmen

1997   Bianco & Cucco: studio in Milan

Memphis: Post Design Gallery in Milan

Moroso: stand at Salone del Mobile and showroom Milan

Cosmit: organization with A. Castiglioni of exhibition dedicated to Giò Ponti and Vico Magistretti

Habitat: small garden house and store in Milan

Kartell: shop in Via Turati, Milan and new corporate identity of the world-wide sales points

Tuffi Duek: refurbishing of showroom New York

Triton: store chain in Brazil

Fontana Arte, Flos, Kartell and Alessi: organization of shopping center "Nimus-Dailam" China in cooperation with Achille Castiglioni

Participation in "Abitare il Tempo 1997" Verona with Ettore Sottsass, Issey Miyake, Achille Castiglioni and Andrea Branzi

Emmemobili: catalogue and stand at Salone del Mobile Milan

è De Padova: set up of shop in C.so Venezia, Milan

Flos: assignment of art direction

1998 Gentry Portofino: refurbishing of showroom Milan

set up of photographical exhibition "Photojeanic" at the "Museum of Contemporary Art" Sao Paulo

Cosmit: project of the Satellite show at the Salone del Mobile Milan

Assoluce: exhibition "Le tecniche e le forme: lampade dal 1946 al 1996" Milan

Moroso: event "One night in heaven" at the showroom in Via Pontaccio, Milan

Flos: display system for lamps, shop in shop at the Ka De We Berlin, shop in Rome, showroom and offices in Paris, stand at Interior Fair '98 Kortrijk

Kartell: office concept (editing of the graphic project and artistic direction of the catalogue), store in New York, Max, logos "KARTELL OFFICE" and "KARTELL CONTRACT"

1999 M Missoni: concept store

Flos: stand at Euroluce Milan, showroom Stockholm

Cosmit: set up of "pavilion 9", creation of the exhibition dedicated to Bruno Munari

Kartell: stand at Salone del Mobile Milan, graphic project and artistic direction of new catalogue, logo, corporate identity, catalogue, graphic interface, data base application and organization of the archive of "Museo d' Impresa Kartell"

Moroso: showroom in Via Pontaccio, Milan, Jorge, 40/80 in collaboration with Achille Castiglioni

Emmemobili: stand at Salone del Mobile Milan, "4" and "12"

Dada Alta Cucina: Quadrante, editing of graphic project and artistic direction of catalogue

Abitare il Tempo: set up of laboratory "Cook Space - food and its instruments, from flavour to form"

"1999: Italia-Europa. Scenari del giovane design": design of general presentation of the area dedicated to "Multimedia Design"

Cosmit: supervising of locations and interior for the fictional program "Ricominciare" produced by RAI

Flos: refurbishing and setting up of the shop C.so Monforte Milan, stand at Light & Building Frankfurt, showroom set up in Milan, Oslo, Copenhagen and Munich, stand at Euroluce Milan

2000 Kartell: stand at Salone del Mobile Milan, showrooms in Milan, Oslo, Copenhagen, Berlin

Moroso: stand at IMM Cologne and Salone del Mobile Milan, showroom of Via Pontaccio, Milan and Ginevra

Emmemobili: Sils, Sandro

Dada Alta Cucina: presentation of kitchens at the Galleria Meravigli, Milan

Abitare il Tempo: exhibition design "Tempo e Abitare". Participation of exhibition "Dafne e il compimento del classico"

Molteni & C.: Biplano

è De Padova: showroom C.so Venezia, Milan

Piombo: showroom Via della Spiga, Milan, graphic project of presentation booklet of showroom

Lectures for Domus Academy Milan

Pandora: assignment of art direction Collections "Pandoramique", "Toy Food" and "Beauty Food"

Foscarini: Supernova

Zani & Zani: Habiby

2001   Flos: stand at Euroluce Milan, shops in Berlin, Düsseldorf, Athens, Istanbul

Moroso: showroom set up Via Pontaccio, Milan

Foscarini: Lenin

Federlegno Arredo: set up of international exhibition "Abitare Italia" in Brasilia

University professor at the Faculty of Design of the Milan Polytechnic

Emmemobili: stand at Salone del Mobile Milan, Sami, Jan

Piombo: coordinated image and set up of Men's Fall/Winter 2001/2002 catwalk collection

Coordination and design of Piombo Casa Collection

Merati: artistic management and coordinated image, stand at Cersaie Bologna

Dolce & Gabbana: beginning of collaboration, concept for the world-wide corner shops, interiors of new headquarters in Milan, interior of a 700 m2 area, dedicated to men's image in C.so Venezia, Milan including furniture and fixtures design for boutique, Martini bar, "Sicilian Barbershop" and grooming area

2002   Flos: assignment of art direction, stands at Light & Building" Frankfurt and Interior exibition in Belgium, showroom in Copenhagen, shop-in-shop systems world-wide

Emmemobili: stand at Salone del Mobile Milan

Palermo, Roma, Lerici, Capri

Kartell: stand at Salone del Mobile Milan, IMM Cologne, ICFF New York

setting up of a specially dedicated space at "Triennale di Milano" for book presentation "Kartell: 150 items, 150 artworks"

New mono-brand showrooms in Cologne, Stockholm, Madrid, Bilbao, Boston, San Francisco, Bologna, Antwerp and Brussels

Fly, Easy

Snaidero: stand at Eurocucina Milan

Moroso: setting up of "Moroso 1952-2002 Off-Scale" exhibition at the Central Railway Station Milan and showroom in Via Pontaccio, Milan

Piombo: mono-brand showroom in Venice, set up of Summer/Winter 2002-2003 catwalk collections, graphic and executive plans for press release

Merati: mono-brand showroom in Via Ventura, Milan, stand at Cersaie Bologna

Cassina: showroom in Via Durini, Milan

2003   Flos: stand at Euroluce Milan, setting up of shop windows, showroom in Belgium, shop-in-shops world-wide

Kartell: stand at Salone del Mobile Milan, mono-brand showrooms in Istanbul, Monaco, Bordeaux, New York

Take, including its packaging

Emmemobili: stand at Salone del Mobile Milan, Shiva, Said, Modular, Dune

Dada Alta Cucina: Vela Quadra

Martini & Rossi: setting up of "Terrazza Martini" at Lido di Venezia during the Venice International Film Festival

Dolce & Gabbana: interior of new boutiques, shop-in-shops and corners world-wide

Society Club: boutique in Montecarlo

2004	Kartell: stand at Salone del Mobile Milan, graphic design for new catalogue
	Bourgie and Four
	Flos: stand at Light & Building Frankfurt, shops world-wide
	Emmemobili: stand at Salone del Mobile Milan, graphic design of invitation cards
	Dolce & Gabbana: interior of new boutiques, shop-in-shops and corners world-wide, new interior concept of boutique dedicated to the women's collection in Via della Spiga, 26 Milan, new interior concept of accessories boutique in Via della Spiga 2, Milan
2005	Molteni & C: "Hi Bridge", "Hi Cove", "Freestyle", "Convivio"
	Foscarini: Teorema
	Swarovski: "Yoga" for the event "Crystal Palace"
	Ceramica Ragno/Marazzi: assignment of art direction, ceramics collection, coordinated image, stand at Cersaie Bologna
	La Rinascente: new concept for the perfumery and accessories area, ground floor in Padua and new Rome Fiume space
	Society Limonta: concept for displaying home wear and accessories, single brand shop in Via Palermo, Milan
	Medea/Mobilidea brand: assignment of art direction, new brand, furniture collection, coordinated image, stand at the Salone del Mobile Milan
2006	Citroen Italia: sales points, stand at the Rimini trade fair, "Kartell-Citroen" event for the Salone del Mobile Milan
	Foscarini: Aretha
	Antonini: concept for jewellery sales points in Tokyo, Fukuoka and Dubai
2006-7	Piper-Heidsieck: pavillion and interior of the new headquarters in Reims
2007	Flos: stand at Euroluce Milan
	Grand Hotel de Bordeaux: Galerie Marchande multibrand space

Photocredits

Pesarini & Michetti
Ruy Teixeira
Walter Gumiero
Santi Caleca
Cristoph Kicherer
Marcus Gaab
Andrea Martiradonna

Acknowledgements

"I would like to thank
all my collaborators, past and present,
as which has been achieved
is also in part due to them;
Rudi Von Wedel, my family
and my loved ones.
Special thanks go to Dr. Claudio Luti.

To Massimo,
Massimo,
Luca
and Eduardo

© 2007 daab
cologne london new york

published and distributed worldwide by
daab gmbh
friesenstr. 50
d - 50670 köln

p + 49 - 221 - 913 927 0
f + 49 - 221 - 913 927 20

mail@daab-online.com
www.daab-online.com

publisher ralf daab
rdaab@daab-online.com

creative director feyyaz
mail@feyyaz.com

layout
ab graphic designer

editorial project by caroline klein
caroline_klein@hotmail.com

caroline klein studied interior design in florence and architecture at
the technical university of munich. she has been working for different
renowned architectural offices as well as a free lance writer, producer
and editor for international architectural magazines and publishers.

introduction by ferruccio laviani

english translation anne kendall, one talk sas milan
french translation dominique florein, one talk sas milan
german translation caroline klein
spanish translation carolina suels
copy editing caroline klein

litho fgv, milan

printed in czech republic
www.graspo.com

isbn 978-3-86654-041-5